green gifts

40 Sustainable and Beautiful Present Ideas

Rosie James and
Claire Cater

Michael O'Mara Books Limited

First published in Great Britain in 2021 by
Michael O'Mara Books Limited
9 Lion Yard
Tremadoc Road
London SW4 7NQ

A CIP catalogue record for this book is available from the British Library.

Papers used by Michael O'Mara Books Limited are natural, recyclable products
made from wood grown in sustainable forests. The manufacturing processes
conform to the environmental regulations of the country of origin.

ISBN: 978-1-78929-321-0 in hardback print format
ISBN: 978-1-78929-322-7 in ebook format

1 2 3 4 5 6 7 8 9 10

This book contains lifestyle advice including instructions and recipes.
Appropriate caution should be used when working with hot or sharp objects.
Neither the publisher nor the author can accept any liability for any injury or
loss that may occur as a result of information given in this book.

Written by Rosie James and Claire Cater
Styled by Claire Cater
Photographed by Vladimir Morozov
Designed by Natasha LeCoultre

Printed and bound in China

www.mombooks.com

CONTENTS

Chapter Three: Plant Power

Chapter Four: Self-Care Treats

Chapter Five: On the Go

Chapter Six: Celebration

Chapter Seven: Pet Presents

Introduction

There is a great power in kindness: it affords the giver respect and the receiver great joy. But that is increased tenfold when you give someone a reusable, home-made gift because you are giving something that is more than physical – you are sowing the seed of sustainability.

You might never truly know the impact you have on those around you when you present them with such a thoughtful gift because what you are actually saying is, 'Hey, you . . . you matter to me.' And not just that, the planet matters too. The upcycled wrapping, the material scraps that are squirrelled away and the abundance of reusable products in your armoury show you care on a global scale. In giving a green gift, you are also giving the gift of a green idea: an eco-friendly inspiration, an organic initiative.

The best thing about the gifts in this collection is that they are all easy to make and cost-effective; you don't need to spend weeks learning a new skill before you can start. The point behind all of these gifts is the idea that you are changing the world by leading by example.

ZERO WASTE, MAXIMUM POTENTIAL / The best way to make sure you have materials at your fingertips to produce eco-friendly gifts is to always be mindful of their usefulness. Collect items like those detailed in the Equipment section at the back of this book and you'll always be able to rustle up a quick eco-gift..

BUYING BETTER / If you are making a gift from this book that requires certain materials that you don't have at home, try to be as resourceful as you can when acquiring them. Look on your local social media pages, which often have a 'regive, reuse, recycle' page, or scour second-hand stores. You can also quite often bulk buy items on eBay at good prices.

It's never too late to make small changes and start living more sustainably, because it's not just the thought that counts, it's also the willingness to be thoughtful that matters.

A NOTE ON SEWING / There are several crafts in here that require either a sewing machine or the ability to hand-sew; if you're not a skilled seamstress already, we recommend YouTube for plenty of tutorials on different kinds of stitches and general techniques.

Eco-Wrapping

'I don't like receiving beautifully wrapped presents,' said no one ever, so pay attention to the finishing touches when it comes to bestowing your green gifts.

Fabric features heavily in this book due to the versatility of its upcycling potential – and because it's readily available and cheap – but it's also an eco-friendly way of wrapping a gift. Follow our step-by-step guide to furoshiki, a Japanese cloth-wrapping technique that's both simple and stunning, as well as a useful way of reusing big or small pieces of material. The key to fabric wrapping is to reuse what you have at home and at your disposal, but if you have to buy new, make sure you opt for organic cotton or other natural fibres, which are biodegradable and therefore non-toxic to Mother Earth.

With wrapping, sometimes less is more if you are going to use patterned fabric or text-strewn paper, but if you are using plain material you have the opportunity to add an extra OMG factor with the accompaniment of a button tie, a sprig of foliage or a pompom or three. Seal the deal with a ceramic heart gift tag or hand-sewn card, and remember: it's always the small pieces that make the big picture.

Wrapping Paper Library

Package up your presents by opting for eco-friendly versions of environmentally damaging, non-recyclable (not to mention bland), shop-bought wrapping paper.

By choosing sustainable gift-wrap options, you're ticking both the budget-conscious and eco-aware boxes. Your home is filled with the perfect materials; you just need to remember to keep them aside. Start a wrap stash that will become a treasure trove of perfect packaging. You can include: old newspapers, magazines, pages from books that are damaged or you no longer read, handwritten letters, old maps, hessian material, recycled fabric and brown/recycled paper.

Tape, as it is made from plastic, falls into the same non-recyclable, zero-benefit category too, so look around for friendlier gift fasteners, such as string, wool, twine, thread, raffia string or even old shoelaces.

Hand-Sewn Cards

These quirky cards are good for any occasion or recipient and can be made into gift tags, too. You'll need card, colourful scrap paper or scraps of fabric, needle and thread (or a sewing machine) and small pieces of washi (paper) tape.

BUNTING CARD / Fold a piece of card. Cut small triangles from either your fabric or scrap paper and arrange in a line across your folded card, securing in place with a little bit of washi tape. Sew along the top of the triangles so your stitching becomes the bunting line. Carefully remove the washi tape once your design is finished.

BUTTERFLIES AND HEARTS CARD / Using the same method as the bunting card, cut out heart or butterfly shapes and secure onto the folded card with the washi tape. Sew down the middle for a fluttering heart or flying butterfly effect. As above, carefully remove the washi tape once your design is finished.

Furoshiki Wrapping

Give your gift in style by using the traditional practice of furoshiki, a Japanese cloth-wrapping technique. Versatile and environmentally friendly, this beautiful method uses pieces of cloth to wrap presents.

HOW TO MAKE

Materials

Any fabric scrap large enough for the gift

Pinking shears if you have them (or fabric scissors if not)

1. Cut the fabric into a square, first checking carefully that it will be large enough for the gift; it needs to be big enough to wrap around the gift from corner to corner. It's better to have more and trim back, so go slowly!

2. Place your present in the centre with your square wrapping fabric in a diamond position. In other words, the corners of the present box should point to the sides of the square.

3. Take one corner of the fabric and fold it over the box, tucking it underneath.

4. Take the opposite corner to the one you have just wrapped and bring it up and over the gift. Fold it neatly underneath itself when it reaches the far edge of the box.

5. Take the remaining two corners, folding the fabric in a little at the closest point to the gift. Bring the two points together over the centre of the present. Tie a knot. If the knot is too big, tie another knot.

TIP

This works best when wrapping a square or boxed gift.

TIP

For smaller gifts, you can avoid using a sewing machine by folding the paper over itself a few times to make the middle secure. You just need to sew the ends together by hand.

Pocket Bags

These gift bags give a hint of mystery and adventure
thanks to the text-filled pages and are perfect for
wrapping a book. Or instead you could use an old map
to give your wanderlust pals a treat within a treat.

HOW TO MAKE

Materials

Old sheet music,
newspaper, pages from
old books, old maps

Sewing machine with
coloured thread

String or twine

Hole punch

1. Take two pieces of paper and sew them together so you have one bigger sheet. Do this as many times as required, depending on the size of gift you want to wrap. For smaller gifts, you can miss out this step entirely.

2. Repeat step 1, so you have two sheets large enough for your gift. Then fold the edges in (to create a neat edge and strengthen the join), put the two pieces together (with the folded edges facing inwards) and sew them together around three edges, leaving one of the shorter edges open.

3. Put your gift inside your paper pocket and fold the top over twice.

4. Make two holes through the folded flap to the back of your packet, thread through some string or twine and tie a bow to fasten the packet.

Bunny Bags

These super-cute bunny-eared paper bags are
perfect not just for Easter-inspired treats but for any
kind of gift for those who love a bit of cuteness.

HOW TO MAKE

Materials

Brown or white paper bags

String

Paper gift tags

Marker pen

1. Pull out the sides of the bag and then flatten it.
   Draw the bunny eyes and nose onto one side of
   the bag.

2. Cut out a V shape from the top of the bag to
   create the ears, making sure you don't go below
   the eyes you have drawn.

3. Pop whatever treats you are adding into the bag
   and stand it up again. Scrunch the two ears up a bit
   to help with shaping them, tie the string around the
   top and pull the two ears out slightly, adding your
   gift tag at the same time.

Finishing Touches

There are lots of ways you can add extra *joie de vivre* to your gift wrap before you hand it over, from the quirky to the elegantly simple. What kind of style reflects your recipient's taste? Set your expectations high and enjoy experimenting with these ideas.

( )) (((((((

ALL BUTTONED UP / Raid your button stash for larger buttons – wooden ones are great for this – and thread them onto some colourful string, tying it together in the centre of your gift.

INITIALS / Perfect if you are using brown paper or something similarly one-colour as a wrap, these eye-catching large letter initials, cut out from scraps of coloured paper, will add a distinctive look to your parcel.

CLAY TAGS / Air-dry clay is great for unique tags, as you can stamp names or initials onto any shapes you want. It's the perfect final touch for fabric wrapping and you can add a sprig or two of your favourite foliage to seal the deal.

POMPOM BOWS / Fun and playful, pompoms are a great way of using up odd bits of leftover wool or yarn you might have. Experiment with size and colours or add a combination of two or three to a simply wrapped parcel. If you're unfamiliar with how to make pompoms, YouTube has a wealth of tutorials!

SECRET POCKETS / Using any leftover scrap paper, cut out two
pieces the same size. Take one piece and begin to wrap the gift as normal
but leave both ends open. Use washi tape to secure the middle in place
and then fold the other piece of paper in half and place the folded end a
third of the way up the present. Fold over the ends of the first piece of
paper and tape in place and then add notes, cards, and a green sprig or
two for colour.

ALL TAPED UP / Washi tape is a traditional Japanese tape made from
paper. It's biodegradable and comes in all manner of designs, colours
and variations, so you'll be spoilt for choice. Stripes of coordinating tape
against a plain background make for a standout look, or cut out shapes
to celebrate specific occasions. It's great for decorating gift tags, too.

Twine Memory Frame

Glass Hand-Soap Bottle

Shibori Cushion Cover

Coiled Vase

Soy-Wax Food Wrap

Sustainable Home

A home should be a collection of things that are loved and treasured, so why not treat new homeowners to purposeful and eco-friendly quirky gifts, like a glass hand-soap bottle, which is both eye-catching and practical. There's nothing basic to see here and thoughtfulness is included with every hand wash!

Giving a relative in need of a quick pick-me-up a bunch of blooms from your garden is sweet but why not put the stems in an easy-to-make coiled vase, too? Then every time they refill it with a new bouquet, they'll be thinking of you.

There are countless changes that can be made in our everyday lives to help protect the environment and these include many mindful swaps around the home, especially when it comes to storing food. The soy-wax food wraps are a reusable solution to keeping produce fresh, so make a bunch in all shapes and sizes for your foodie squad and show them a great eco-alternative to plastic food wrap.

Twine Memory Frame

This is such a simple yet fun way to display photos or messages without a drawing pin or magnet in sight. Why not use it to display memories from a fabulous holiday or fill it with your favourite snaps of you and your partner as a special anniversary gift?

HOW TO MAKE

Materials

Empty picture frame

Paint and paint brush, if you want to change the colour of your photo frame (use pots that you have already, like left-over white emulsion)

Mini wooden pegs (as many as you want, depending on the number of photos you want displayed)

Brightly coloured twine in two different colours (enough to criss-cross the frame many times)

Small tack nails and a hammer

1. If you want to make the coloured twine that your photos will hang from really stand out, you could give your old photo frame a coat or two of white paint.

2. Once the frame has dried, fix nails around the back of the frame, spacing them unevenly to make the string pattern more interesting.

3. Using one continuous piece, zigzag your twine across the back in an overlapping fashion by wrapping it around each nail and pulling it taut as you go. Then tie off the twine on the last nail.

4. Do the same with your other twine until you have a good mesh of super-bright string across your frame.

5. Now simply clip on some mini wooden pegs to display some cute photos or drawings on your new memo board, or slot them into the string pattern.

TIP

*Fill up your fancy
bottles with soap or
shampoo at your local
zero-waste shop.*

Glass Hand-Soap Bottle

Fancy drinks bottles often feel too pretty to recycle, so
why not turn them into hand soap or shampoo dispensers
instead and keep them on display for all to see?

▲ ▲ ▲ ▲ ▲

HOW TO MAKE

Materials

Empty glass bottle

Water-based sealant (optional)

Paint brush (optional)

Pump dispenser/nozzles
saved from toiletries you
have already used

1. Take the empty bottle of your choice and, using your paint brush, apply a water-based sealant so it covers both the labels on the front and the back of the bottle, if you're leaving them on – if not, scrub them off and skip this step. These bottles will get wet and soapy regularly, so you want a good coverage of the sealant (approximately four layers) all over the edges of the label and onto the bottle.

2. Once that is dry, choose the right dispenser to fit your bottle. Most dispenser pumps are a standard-fit size and come in a range of finishes. You might need to trim the interior straw of the nozzle depending on the depth of your glass bottle.

3. Fill your bottle with the liquid of choice and it's all ready to use. As well as being a talking point, it's also a quirky and eco-friendly housewarming gift.

Shibori Cushion Cover

This is a super-simple way to jazz up an old piece of plain white material to create a beautiful accent in your living space. Shibori is a Japanese technique of dying, meaning to 'wring out', though you probably know it as tie-dye! The dye we suggest here is turmeric, which will create a beautiful sunshine-inspired pattern, perfect for helping the recipient of your gift wake up with a smile. Just make sure to keep the cushion out of direct sunlight to prevent fading.

HOW TO MAKE

Materials

An old square cushion (or cushion inner) in need of some love

1 piece of white organic cotton fabric (see calculation in step 1)

1 tbsp turmeric powder

Water

Large stainless-steel saucepan

Elastic bands

Iron

Sewing machine

Pins

1. Measure your cushion. The height of your fabric will be the same as the pillow itself, and the width will be the width of your cushion multiplied by 2.25 (to allow for the overlap).

2. Concertina fold the fabric into a long strip. Tightly wrap elastic bands at intervals along this strip.

3. Make your dye bath by adding 1 tbsp of turmeric powder to 1 litre (0.2 gallons) of water in a saucepan for a bright sunshine-yellow colour.

4. Heat the water slowly until it's simmering and then add your fabric strip so it's fully submerged in the pot.

5. Leave to soak on the lowest heat for forty minutes. Remove the fabric from the dye bath, squeezing any excess water out. Take off the elastic bands and rinse before allowing the fabric to dry naturally.

6. Hem the two short edges by folding and pressing in 1cm (just under ½in) each side and sewing along next to the raw edge of the fabric.

7. With the fabric lying lengthways, right side (i.e. the side you want on the outside of the case) up, fold the short sides in towards the middle, overlapping at the centre, to give an overall width 2.5cm (1in) less than the height. You should now have an almost-square that is ever so slightly taller than it is wide, with the right side of the fabric inside (i.e. your almost-cushion-cover is inside-out).

8. Pin in place and then sew along the open edges at the top and bottom. You don't need to leave an opening as you have created one already where the fabric overlaps. Trim any excess fabric from the corners, then turn the right way out and finish by putting in your old cushion or inner.

Coiled Vase

The versality of these coiled containers make them ideal gifts,
as they can be made into vases, trinket bowls or any other
cylindrical vessel of your choice. As a vase, the bare cord
punctuated by coloured threads is a simple yet classic and stylish
way to show off freshly picked blooms from your garden.

HOW TO MAKE

Materials

An old glass jar – this will
determine the size of your vase

Cotton cord approximately
4mm (less than ¼in) in
thickness – you will need
approximately 6m (19ft)
for a medium-sized vase

Embroidery thread or
wool in a colour of your
choice – whatever you have
in your craft stash, as this
is a great way to use it up
(we used 6 skeins of thread
around 7–8m (25ft) a skein
for a vase 15cm (6in) tall)

Large darning needle

1. Thread your needle with a length of embroidery
yarn that you find manageable to work with and tie
a knot in the end.

2. Take the end of the cotton cord and wind it
tightly into a coil so the end is tucked neatly into
the centre. You only need to make a small ring
(approximately two to three strings wide) initially.

3. Pass the needle through the coil and out the other
side and then pass the needle back into the coil at
a right angle to you first thread. (See photo
'a' overleaf.)

4. Now the centre of the coil is secure, take your
needle and stitch over the top of two rings and
down through the gap between it and the next coil.
(See photo 'b' overleaf.)

TIP

If you want to give your vase a narrow neck, you will need to put your glass jar inside before you start narrowing the coils.

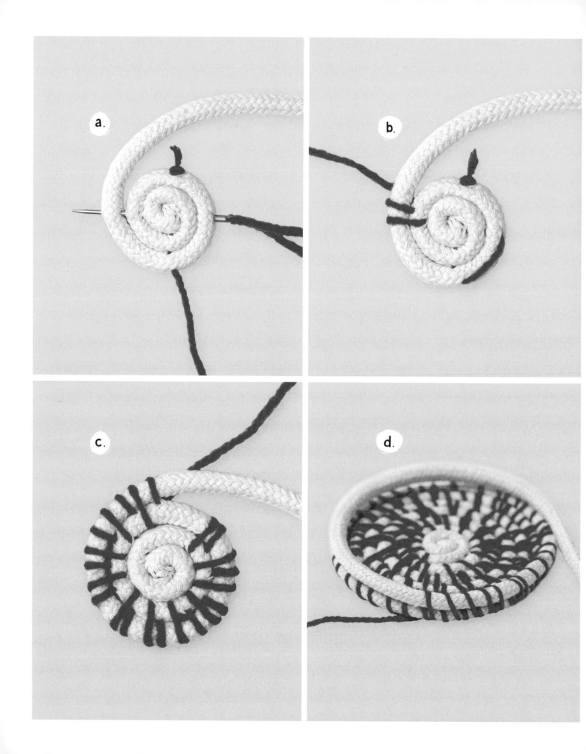

5. Your next stitch only needs to connect one coil and so, instead of passing the needle down between two rings, let it catch a little bit of the second ring of cord and pull it through. This will help make your vase sturdy. (See photo 'b'.)

6. Continue winding the cord around in a spiral and working your way around the coil with the embroidery thread as it grows, alternating stitches so that one stitch goes over one piece of cord (catching the stitch next to it) and the next stitch goes over two. (See photo 'c'.)

7. When you have coiled your base so that it is big enough for your glass container to sit on top of, begin to coil the cord up the sides. Your first side coil will need to have all the stitches wrapped around both pieces of cord – the base and the first layer. (See photo 'd'.)

8. After you have gone around once, you can go back to alternate stitching, making sure that every other stitch passes through the cord coiled below it.

9. When you have gone as high as your glass container, look back at the base of your coil and find the point where you started to bring your cord up to make the side wall. Your very top bit of cord should finish directly above that.

10. Cut the cord at a slight angle and continue your stitching until the end is secured. Tie a knot at the end of your thread and then pass the thread between two pieces of cord so it's hidden. Slide your glass jar in and fill with flowers!

Soy-Wax
Food Wrap

An ideal way to cover and protect food produce, soy-wax wraps are completely sustainable and natural – a winning alternative to plastic. They are quick to make from your favourite funky material and usable straight away.

HOW TO MAKE

Materials

Organic cotton fabric
30cm x 20cm (12in x 8in)

Soy wax, 10–15g
(½–¾oz) per wrap

Baking paper

Baking tray

Old paint brush

Pinking shears (optional)

1. If you are using the soy-wax wrap to cover leftovers, draw on the fabric around the bowls or dishes you wish to cover and mark an extra 2–3cm (1in) around the template so that the fabric fully covers and folds over the edges of the dish. You can also just make multi-purpose square wraps.

2. Cut the fabric using pinking shears if you have them. Normal fabric scissors will work but pinking shears are ideal as they will help prevent the fabric from fraying.

3. Preheat your oven to 90°C (180°F) and line a flat oven tray with baking paper. Lay your fabric on the tray and sprinkle the soy wax over the top, aiming for a light, even covering. You can always add more wax later.

4. Put the tray in the oven for a couple of minutes and monitor the melting wax, taking it out when it has all melted.

5. Using your old paintbrush, spread the wax across the fabric so there is an even coverage on all the material. If a few areas have only a thin covering, add more wax drops and return to the oven.

6. Hang your soy-wax wrap up to dry. Once it has solidified, it is ready to use. To wash soy-wax wraps in between uses, rinse with cool or lukewarm water and eco-friendly washing-up liquid – never use hot water.

TIP

The warmth from your hands will make the wax wrap malleable – press the edges together to seal around the item you are wrapping.

Avocado Plant and Washi Tape Pot

Potted Ginger Plant

Cute Clay Pots

Hanging Mini Succulents

Pressed-Bloom Picture

Jar Terrarium

Plant Power

Bring the wild inside and be inspired by Mother Nature with some home-grown greenery and produce. Ginger has a long list of health-boosting properties, so it's an ideal plant present for all your health-conscious pals. Avocado is also a superfood, making it top of our list of desirable plants to grow and give.

Bringing plants into a home, like those described in the hanging mini succulents tutorial, will bring a wealth of benefits to your world. Succulents are not just aesthetically pleasing but also require minimal care and attention.

We all know that nature feeds the soul, plus having plants in your home can help purify the air around you by absorbing pollutants. They are also proven to help increase your focus as well as having anxiety-reducing benefits, which makes them perfect for a stressed-out loved one. Pop a home-grown plant in a personalized pot as a gift of luck and vitality. Or if you have a pal who likes a minimalist style, bring a tiny touch of nature to their lives with the quirky jar terrarium.

TIP

If you have an old terracotta or other plain-coloured pot at home, these will also work — just make sure they are clean so the tape will adhere.

Avocado Plant and Washi Tape Pot

Growing your own avocado plant is a cheap and eco-friendly way of making sure you don't just discard the pit of this nutritious and flavoursome fruit.

HOW TO MAKE

Materials

Avocado pit

3 cocktail sticks

Small glass jar (condiment jars work well)

Soil for planting

White plant pot

Washi tape in colours and patterns of your choice (at least two colours works well)

Waterproof sealant

For the plant:

1. The shape of your avocado pit might vary but all pits will have a slightly flat bottom, from which the roots will grow, and a top, which is pointier, from which the sprout will grow.

2. Take three cocktail sticks and push them into the side of the pit at a slightly upward angle, evenly spaced out, sloping away from the base. They will need to be in quite firmly, as they form a scaffold that will allow you to rest the bottom of your avocado pit in water.

3. Take your pit and place it in a small glass jar so that the bottom is half submerged in water. If you use a clear glass, you can see when the roots start to grow and when you need to change the water (approximately every five days or so to prevent fungus growth).

4. Over the next six to eight weeks, your avocado pit will split open and a tiny tap root will emerge from the bottom. It's important to always make sure the roots are completely submerged in water.

5. Eventually you will see a small sprout appear out of the top of your avocado pit. If you are feeling brave, when the stem is about 15cm (6–7in) tall, cut it back to about half its length, as this encourages the plant to regrow bushier.

6. Remove it from the water and plant it in rich humus soil, leaving the top half of the pit exposed.

7. Place your avocado plant on a windowsill and make sure it gets plenty of sun and water frequently. This is a beautiful house plant and who knows, maybe one day you'll be rewarded with fruit as a bonus!

For the pot:

8. Plan a design for your washi tape first so that you know exactly how you are going to cut and stick the tape onto your pot.

9. Be creative! The smaller the pieces of tape, the fiddlier, but you will find it gives an abstract, mosaic look.

10. You will need a small amount of waterproof sealant to protect your design. Apply three or four thin layers to your pot, leaving it to dry for a couple of hours between each coat.

11. When it's all dry, you are ready to add soil and place your avocado plant into its beautiful new home.

Potted Ginger Plant

Growing your own superfood is like having your own superpower so giving a ginger plant as a gift is particularly thoughtful. Add a colourful tassel fringe to your plant pot to finish the look in a vibrant, jazzy style.

HOW TO MAKE

Materials

Organic ginger root

Potting compost

Straight-edged plant pot, at least 35cm (14in) wide

Cotton cord approximately 3mm ('/8in) thick in different colours (you will need roughly 20x the circumference of your pot – or more, if your cord is thinner)

Comb

For the plant:

1. If you don't already have ginger root at home, choose some that is around the size of your thumb from a local organic health food shop. Look for some that has pale pointy growth buds, or eyes, already forming. If you are buying from a supermarket, you may want to soak your ginger overnight in water, as it is often treated with chemicals that inhibit new growth.

2. Once you are happy your ginger has a couple of growth buds (if soaking in water doesn't produce any, leave it on a windowsill for a couple of days until you see a bud form on the surface), take your large, wide pot and fill with a good potting soil. Place your ginger in the soil with the growth 'eyes' facing up, covering it with 2–3cm (1in) of soil.

3. Ginger thrives in partial sunlight, so put your pot in a place with morning sun if possible and keep the soil well watered but not soggy. A good way to make sure you're not overwatering is to mist the soil.

For the pot:

4. Take any colour cord and wrap it around the top of your plant pot one and a half times, cut to length and lay it on your worksurface. Cut shorter pieces of cord slightly longer than twice the length you want your tassel to be (we cut 13cm (5in) lengths, and used just over a hundred of them for this pot) and lay them next to the long strip.

5. Beginning 5cm (2in) in from one end, start adding your tassels by folding the shorter lengths of cord in half, placing the loop underneath the main cord and bringing the two loose ends over the top of the long cord and through the loop, forming a 'lark knot'.

6. Decide on what sort of colourful pattern you want for your fringe and add tassels in the same way as above until you have covered almost the entire circumference of the pot.

7. When you have added almost enough tassels, stop – do not add the last few. Wrap it around the top of your pot and tie the two ends of the cord in a tight knot to secure the tassel fringe tightly around the pot, take it back off and then add the last few tassels to cover up the knot.

8. Separate the cotton cord strands with a comb to form the tassels, trim with scissors to neaten them, then shimmy the cord back onto the pot.

TIP

Ginger plants won't be rushed, so it will most likely take at least five months for these slowpokes to become beautiful plants.

Cute Clay Pots

These cunning clay pots aren't just simple and easy to make but they also represent such a unique and individual eco gift that they should be renamed 'the perfect pot'! The geometric design can be adapted to suit the size and purpose of your pot. Why not use them as a handy pencil holder, a sleek planter for a pretty shrub or fill one with wrapped chocolates as a treat for a sweet-toothed friend?

▲ ▲ ▲ ▲ ▲

HOW TO MAKE

Materials

Air-dry clay

Sharp knife

Chopping board

Waterproof sealant (if using as a plant pot)

1. Decide what size pot you want to make and pull away a chunk of clay slightly bigger than you want the finished product to be. Roll the clay for about five minutes, as the more you handle the clay, the more air bubbles you will push out. Make your clay into a ball shape.

2. Push your thumbs into the centre of the ball of clay and pinch between your fingers and thumb to form a bowl shape that has a solid base and thick sides. If you are going to use your pot for a plant, this is the time to make a small drainage hole in the base.

3. Let your clay dry for twenty-four hours. You need the clay to be firm but soft enough for you to cut slices from it. If the clay sticks to the knife when you are cutting, let your pot dry for another couple of hours.

4. Once you are happy that your pot is ready to work with, pop it on your chopping board, take your knife and cut away a good straight bottom, so your pot has an even base, and then cut straight slices into the side to create geometric facets. You might want to use a smaller knife to add smaller cuts to the rim.

5. When you are happy with your design, let your pot completely dry out. This can take several days, but you will know it is fully dry when the colour has changed from grey to white and it feels nice and solid.

6. If you are going to put a plant in your pot you will need a small amount of waterproof sealant to protect the clay. Apply a thin layer to your pot, inside and out, and leave to dry for a couple of hours. When it is dry, apply another layer and repeat until you have built up three or four layers. When it's completely dry, you are ready to add soil and your plant.

Hanging
Mini Succulents

These pots, combined with these tassel hangers, are the perfect
home for your succulents and will bring a fresh, miniature-
garden look to your wall. Nature-loving friends will treasure
a graceful pair of plants as a simple, stimulating gift.

HOW TO MAKE

Materials

Air-dry clay

Sharp knife

Cord or string thick enough
to support the plant pot

Colourful embroidery threads

Small bowl

Sandpaper

Potting soil suitable
for succulents

Succulents

1. The size of your pots will depend on your succulent
   sizes, so make sure you have those before you start.

2. Roll out the air-dry clay until it is about 0.5cm (under
   ¼in) thick and place it into a small bowl, pushing it
   smoothly against the inside of your bowl-mould to
   ensure there are no wrinkles. Trim the top edge
   with a knife so it is neat and even.

3. Leave the clay to dry. It should come out of the
   mould easily when it is fully dry. If it doesn't, leave it
   to dry for longer or try very gently breaking the seal
   with a sharp knife. Use sandpaper to lightly smooth
   out any rough edges. Do this outside or by a window
   so you don't inhale the clay dust.

4. Cut two identical lengths of cord to the length you want your hanger to be. Then cut a third cord that is 20cm (8in) longer (or longer if you want a bigger loop). Add washi tape to one end of each cord to prevent fraying. Gather the three lengths together, folding the end of the longer one over to form a loop. Secure with a small piece of scrap thread (we will cover it up later).

5. Take your first coloured thread and tie it to the cord just below the loop. Start wrapping it around the three cords nice and tightly and then add as many other coloured threads as you like, depending on your desired pattern. Make sure you go far enough up to cover and secure where the end of the loop joins the rest of the cords (this will also conceal the thread from step 4). Tie a knot in the last bit of thread and, using a needle, sew the loose end in for a neat finish.

6. Decide how far down the hanger you want your pot to rest and tie a coloured piece of thread around the cords at that point, like you did at the top of the hanger. Repeat this wrapping again to create your pattern, and knot and sew through the thread to finish again.

7. Cut the remaining cord to the length you want so it's even – if you haven't cut the washi tape off with the ends, remove it. If you would like a tasselled look, unravel the strands below the wrapping.

TIP

You can also use these tassel hangers to display the geometric Cute Clay Pots from page 46.

Pressed-Bloom Picture

A personalized frame of pressed flowers is a thoughtful and intimate gift that can provide everlasting memories of a special occasion.

HOW TO MAKE

Materials

Wild flowers or leaves of your choice

Baking paper

Heavy books

Old picture frame

A piece of nice fabric very slightly larger than your frame, e.g. unbleached cotton

1. Pick a selection of your favourite wild flowers and place them between two sheets of baking paper.

2. Put the paper and flowers between the pages of a heavy book so that they all have equal pressure and leave for at least a week so they can dry out – ideally two.

3. Once the flowers are sufficiently pressed, remove them from the book and lay them out ready to frame.

4. Take the photo frame and carefully remove and clean the glass. Lay the flowers face down on the glass to create an attractive arrangement.

5. Carefully lay the backing fabric over the flowers, being careful not to dislodge them. Fit the back of the frame on tightly and your flowers will stay in place. If it feels like there is a little too much space in the frame to allow your arrangement to stay in place, add a couple of layers of paper behind the fabric to fill this out and keep everything secure.

Jar Terrarium

A miniature garden in a jar is a fresh way of bringing a bit of wildlife inside and makes a unique, eco-friendly gift for nature lovers.

▲ ▲ ▲ ▲ ▲

HOW TO MAKE

Materials

A clean, air-tight jar

A variety of moss – the best place to gather it is in a moist and shady area (only take what you need, always leaving enough behind)

Tiny high-humidity-tolerant plants (optional)

Small pebbles or gravel

Compost

Decorative objects – rocks, shells, acorn caps, etc.

Helpful tools: tweezers, chopstick, a teaspoon

Rainwater in a spray bottle/plant mister

1. Clean the small pebbles and add them into the jar to make a base drainage layer of around 1cm (½in).

2. Add a 1cm (½in) layer of compost on top of the gravel and use a tool to compress it down.

3. Arrange your moss, plants and any decorative items. Once you are happy with your design, use a chopstick to press them firmly into the soil.

4. Mist the jar walls with a couple of sprays of water and seal the jar. You can always add more water later if it seems too dry. If you've added too much, leave the lid off for a day or two to let some moisture escape.

5. Place your new terrarium in a well-lit area, away from direct sunlight. Your terrarium will naturally mist up and clear in cycles as your plants breathe and photosynthesize. If you have no condensation or too much, add or remove moisture accordingly.

TIP

You may need to
change the depth of your
pebble, soil and moss layers
depending on the size of
your chosen vessel; aim
for roughly two thirds
empty space.

Espresso Exfoliation

Reusable Face Pads

Drawstring Pouch

Herbal Bath Bombs

Soothing Eye Mask

Grapefruit Hand Cream

Nourishing Lip Balm

Self-care is important, and this soothing eye mask will work wonders if you or a friend need a bit of extra help getting some shut-eye. The relaxing lavender in this easy-to-make mask has anxiety-reducing properties and a calming scent.

Your loved ones will never throw away coffee grounds again after they see them in action as they rejuvenate their complexion with an espresso exfoliation facial. Reusable face pads are also so simple and cheery to make, not to mention eco-friendly, that chances are, if you gift some to skincare-obsessed pals, too, you'll be seeing them all over Instagram before you can wipe off that last drop of cleanser.

And for a perfect holdall to store all your personal pampering essentials, like the nourishing homemade lip balm or super-soft hand cream, look no further than the drawstring pouch. Rummage through your old clothes or tablecloths for some vibrant fabric and get busy sewing up a personalized beauty bag for a friend in need.

Self-Care Treats

Espresso Exfoliation

The beauty of this exfoliating mask is in its simplicity:
a collagen-boosting scrub made with the leftover
coffee grounds from your morning pick-me-up.

‖‖‖‖‖‖‖‖

HOW TO MAKE

Ingredients

1 tbsp used coffee grounds

1 tbsp oil of your
choice (see step 1)

Old jar to store

1. Add your used coffee grounds to a bowl and mix with oil of your choice. Olive oil is good for dry skin; alternatively, choose rosehip for its renewal properties or jojoba to promote softer skin.

2. Apply the mixture in a circular motion to your face (you could use the reusable face pads from page 62). The coffee grounds act as an exfoliant to help unblock pores and rejuvenate your complexion while still being gentle enough for sensitive skin.

3. Once you have covered all areas of your face and neck, rinse away with warm water.

4. Store in an old jar with an air-tight lid and keep in the fridge for up to one month. We would recommend using this once or twice a week.

TIP

Try using vitamin E oil and adding a drop or two of Frankincense essential oil to the scrub for a moisturizing finish.

TIP

Why not pile up the pads and wrap in string for a stylish present for beauty-conscious friends.

Reusable Face Pads

An eco-friendly addition to any skincare routine, these reusable face pads are super fast to make.

HOW TO MAKE

Materials

Pieces of organic cotton fabric, such as old shirts or bedsheets – anything with a pattern works well

1 or 2 flannels (wash cloths made from towelling)

Sewing machine or needle and thread

Paper

Iron

1. Measure a 9cm (3½in) diameter circle on a piece of scrap paper, cut it out and use it as a template to cut circles from the cotton and flannel.

2. Take a circle of cotton and one of flannel and put the right (i.e. outer) sides of your fabrics together. Pin the layers together.

3. With a sewing machine or by hand, stitch round the circle, 6mm (¼in) from the edge. Leave a 2.5cm (1in) gap so you can turn the material the right way out after sewing the edges. Turn the fabric right way out and give it a quick press with a hot iron.

4. Topstitch around the pressed circle, again 6mm (¼in) from the edge. This will close up the gap you left and give a neat finish.

5. Use your normal cleanser on the flannel side of these pads just as you would a cotton wool pad.

Drawstring Pouch

This multi-purpose drawstring bag can be adapted
to suit each recipient's needs and taste.

|||||||||||

HOW TO MAKE

Materials

2 pieces 25cm x 33cm
(10in x 13in) organic
cotton fabric

2 ties, 45cm (18in) in
length – you can use ribbon,
cord, string – anything
that isn't too thick

Safety pin

Sewing machine or
needle and thread

Pinking shears (optional)

Pins

Iron

1. Take one piece of fabric and, right side (i.e. the side you want to be the outside of the bag) down, turn over 6mm (¼in) at the top and fold it towards you. Iron down the turnover so it sits flat. Do the same for both pieces of fabric.

2. Now you have a top hem for each, put the right sides of the material together and lay flat. Mark 5cm (2in) from the top on the left and right edge of the fabric (you can pin them together if you like). Use a sewing machine or hand-sew 2.5cm (1in) from the left edge, starting at the mark you made, going down the left-hand side, along the bottom and up the right-hand side, stopping at the second mark you made. (See photo 'a' overleaf.)

3. Open the bag up and fit it over the end of an ironing board to iron the side slits (see photo 'b' overleaf) and then iron the material flat open. Take the (side) edge that you have pressed and fold it under and then press it again, making sure both edges are turned under. Do the same on the other side opening, too.

TIP

Why not play around with clashing colours and pick a drawstring that contrasts strongly with the main fabric to give your bag that wow factor.

a.

b.

c.

d.

4. Stitch the side opening along the folded edges you have made from the top to the bit that has already been sewn 5cm (2in) down, across the seam between the two pieces of fabric and then back up again to the top. Trim any excess thread you have. (See photo 'b'.)

5. With the bag in a flat position again, fold down the top edges about 2.5cm (1in) and pin in place. Stitch along one side at a time. (See photo 'c'.)

6. Use pinking shears (or scissors) to trim any excess fabric and then turn your bag right side out. Take one length of ribbon or string, fold over the end and put the safety pin through it. Thread the safety pin and attached string through the tube you have created, along one side, flip the bag over and send it back along the other side so both ends of the string finish at the same side. Take your other piece of string and repeat the process, starting at the opposite side of the bag than before, so that you end up with two string ends on each side. (See photo 'd'.)

7. Tie the two ends on either side into small knots (effectively creating two loops of string with a knot on each side of the bag) and then pull on them to test the drawstring mechanism of your new bag.

Herbal Bath Bombs

A detoxifying treat that is sure to relax even the most frazzled friend, these bath bombs' lavender and peppermint scents are soothing for the mind while the Epsom salts do the same for the skin.

HOW TO MAKE

Materials

(makes 8 small bath bombs)

120g (4½oz) baking (bicarbonate of) soda

65g (2¾oz) Epsom salts

60g (2½oz) citric acid

1 tsp oil (olive, almond and sunflower all work well)

½ tsp lavender essential oil

Silicone ice cube tray

Water in a spray bottle

Handful of dried and crushed peppermint leaves, lavender flowers and flower petals

1. Sprinkle some dried peppermint and lavender leaves into your silicone tray moulds as they will add decoration to the top of your bath bombs.

2. Put the baking soda, citric acid and Epsom salts in a bowl and whisk together, adding in the oil and essential oil, too.

3. Spray your mixture with 2–3 pumps of water and continue to mix. Using your hands to test the texture, continue to spray more water until you have a mixture the consistency of slightly wet sand. You don't want it to be too wet, just damp enough to hold form when you squeeze it in your hand.

4. Spoon a tablespoon of your mixture into a mould on top of the dried flowers and press down slightly.

5. Scatter a layer of dried peppermint on top, making sure you have a nice distribution around the edges, then spoon another tablespoon of mixture on top of that.

6. Press the mixture down firmly, smoothing away any fingerprint marks and decorate with more peppermint leaves.

7. Leave to harden for twenty-four hours and then carefully pop the bath bombs out of the silicone tray.

8. Store in a glass jar and, if they're a gift, add a stylish fabric covering over the lid.

TIP

If you want to get even fancier, you can infuse your oil with calendula petals for that extra touch of opulence.

TIP

If you prefer some cold therapy on your peepers, pop it in the freezer for ten minutes to cool.

Soothing Eye Mask

Perfect for a pampered power nap or for a friend who wants to bring the luxurious feeling of a spa into their home.

HOW TO MAKE

Materials

2 pieces of 24cm x 11cm (9½in x 4½in) cotton fabric

160g (⅔ cup) jasmine rice

12g (⅓ cup) dried lavender

Sewing machine or needle and thread

1. Take the two pieces of your chosen fabric and place the right sides of the fabric together.

2. On a machine (or by hand using backstitch), sew around the fabric approximately 6mm (¼in) from the edge. Don't go all the way around the rectangle; make sure you leave a 5cm (2in) gap on one of the shorter sides to add your filling.

3. Cut the corners off your fabric, being careful not to cut the stitching, and then turn your rectangle the right way out.

4. Fill your pillow with the dried lavender and jasmine rice and then sew the opening shut.

5. To heat your eye mask, pop it in the microwave for 30 seconds at a time until it's warm enough (be careful that it doesn't overheat).

Grapefruit Hand Cream

This luxurious hand butter that melts into the skin and moisturizes your parched hands is an effortless gift to make.

( )) (( ) ( )) (

HOW TO MAKE

Materials

85g (3½oz) coconut oil

50g (2oz) mango butter (or you could opt for shea or cocoa butter if you prefer)

28g (1oz) olive or almond oil

3.5g (1.5 tbsp) soy wax

10 drops skin-friendly grapefruit essential oil

Whisk

Used moisturizer tub

1. Put all the ingredients except for the essential oil in a bowl and either pop it into the microwave or heat slowly over a saucepan of boiling water.

2. Once all the ingredients have melted together, take it off the heat and add the grapefruit essential oil.

3. Leave your mixture to cool in the fridge for three to four hours, or on the side overnight, until the mixture is soft but solid.

4. Using an electric or hand-held whisk, whisk the mixture for 2–10 minutes until it starts to whip (this will of course be much quicker with an electric whisk than by hand!).

5. Once it has all whipped up and it doesn't drop easily from the whisk, you are ready to put it in a container of your choice. Or start slathering it straight onto your grateful hands!

TIP

If the cream isn't thickening up, try putting it in the fridge for 10 minutes and trying again.

Nourishing Lip Balm

Moisturizing? Check. Protective? Check. This sustainable and plant-based lip balm will be a welcome addition to pouts everywhere thanks to its soft, protective qualities. It is an inexpensive yet essential gift that will guard and nourish your recipient's lips so that they are supple, strong and kissable. Mwah!

HOW TO MAKE

Materials

20g (¾oz) soy wax

14g (½oz) coconut oil

20g (¾oz) shea butter

10 to 12 drops skin-friendly peppermint essential oil

Small glass pots or tins (e.g. from lip balms you've used up) or cardboard lip-balm tubes

1. Put the soy wax in a bowl over a pan of hot water on the stove. When it has all melted, add in the shea butter and coconut oil and continue to stir until it has completely melted and combined.

2. Stir in 10 to 12 drops of the peppermint essential oil and then remove from the heat.

3. Pour or syringe your mixture into your containers.

4. Leave the lip balm to set for twenty-four hours and then it should be perfect to apply.

These eco-friendly gifts are perfect for those everyday items that no longer need to be single use. Each has a touch of personality, too, making them thoughtful, functional and unique accessories.

The bento lunch sack will keep al fresco-dining fans super happy, as they can tie up and carry their munchies out on a hike. Or, if you are being a little less energetic, pack it with a treat or two for a late brunch. The handy fabric bookmark not only looks divine but, with its pen-holder pocket, will also keep even the most eager reader in their element. Travel enthusiasts, meanwhile, can keep all their mementos and souvenirs in the travel folder of the gods. We also love the unique tassel keyring, which can brighten up any drab bag or help out with the daily lost-your-car-keys dilemma.

In fact, all these gifts will be welcome, whether the recipient is constantly on the go, trying to plan their next adventure or simply has more than one book/journal/diary in need of their attention. You might as well call them practically perfect.

On the Go

Bento Lunch Sack

The perfect eco-friendly sack for your lunch, this will be an everlasting gift to fill with edible delights for your foodie friends.

HOW TO MAKE

Materials

2 triangular pieces of fabric,
58cm x 58cm x 80cm
(23in x 23in x 31½in)

Sewing machine

1. Depending on the fabric you are using, you may wish to zigzag stitch along the edges to stop any fraying. To join the triangles together, lay them flat, right side up so the right-angle points are facing each other (the longer edges are on the outside). Move one piece over the top of the other so that the point is touching the centre of the long edge of the triangle underneath (see photo 'a').

2. Sew a straight line across the centre of the triangles from right-angle to right-angle and then sew around the edges where the two triangles overlap and there are two layers of fabric. This will form a diamond shape. The aim is to have no 'pockets', leaving you with just one piece of material. (See photo 'a'.)

3. Now fold the bag in half so that the points are aligned with right sides (i.e. the outside of the bag) together. Pin in place. You are now going to sew the right and left sides together but stop about 8cm (3½in) from the bottom of either side and sew across the corners (see photo 'b').

TIP

If you're feeling confident on the sewing machine, try using a contrasting colour thread as a design feature.

4. Once you have sewn both sides and the corner sections, cut the corners off, not too close to the stitching and turn right side out. Iron your bag, fill with whatever takes your fancy and knot or double-knot to finish.

a.

b.

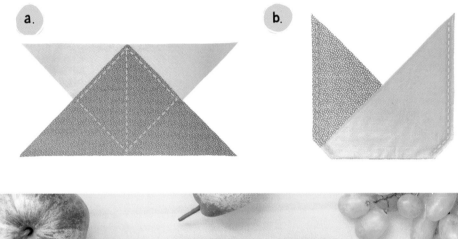

Pen Pocket Bookmark

For book devourers who always have a different tale on the go,
this everlasting page-marker is not just a pretty alternative to
ear-marking your favourite yarn, the handy pen compartment
and added elastic also make it a practical, useful gift for those
who like to keep a journal or diary. Our gift will fit an A4 notebook
but you can amend the size to suit your lucky recipient's needs.

HOW TO MAKE

Materials

2 strips of fabric, 6cm x
20cm (2½in x 8in) for
the bookmark strips

I strip of fabric, 6cm x
25cm long (2½in x 10in)
for the pocket strip

I piece of elastic, 2.5 cm
x 35cm (1in x 14in)

Sewing machine or
needle and thread

Pins

Iron

1. Fold the pocket strip in half across the width so the right sides (i.e. the sides you want visible) of the material are on the outside and then iron flat. Stitch across the folded edge (not the edge where the two ends meet) about 6mm (¹/₄in) in.

2. Now you need to stack all the bits of fabric together. Start with one of the bookmark strips, right side up. Then put your pocket piece on top of that, right side up so that the end you have stitched is near the middle.

3. Put the elastic on top, aligning the raw edges on the right side, making sure it is fairly central (see photo 'a' overleaf) and then finally add the remaining bookmark strip, right side down, and pin all the layers in place.

4. Leaving a 6mm (¼in) seam allowance, sew around the edge of the bookmark, leaving the bottom open where the elastic is sticking out. Make sure you backstitch at the start and end or your stiches will come loose when you turn it out. (See photo 'b'.)

5. Trim the corners now and then turn the bookmark right side out using a chopstick or pen to help push out the corners.

6. Tuck in the open edge at the bottom and iron the bookmark flat. Then push the other end of the elastic into the open end of the bookmark, making sure the elastic isn't twisted. Topstitch along the bottom of the bookmark to hold the elastic in place and then continue to topstitch around the whole bookmark. (See photo 'c'.)

7. Finish by sewing a line down the middle of just the pocket section to make two pen or pencil sections and then pop around a notebook or journal.

TIP

To make the present extra-special, why not pick out some pretty pens to slip inside the pocket before you gift it?

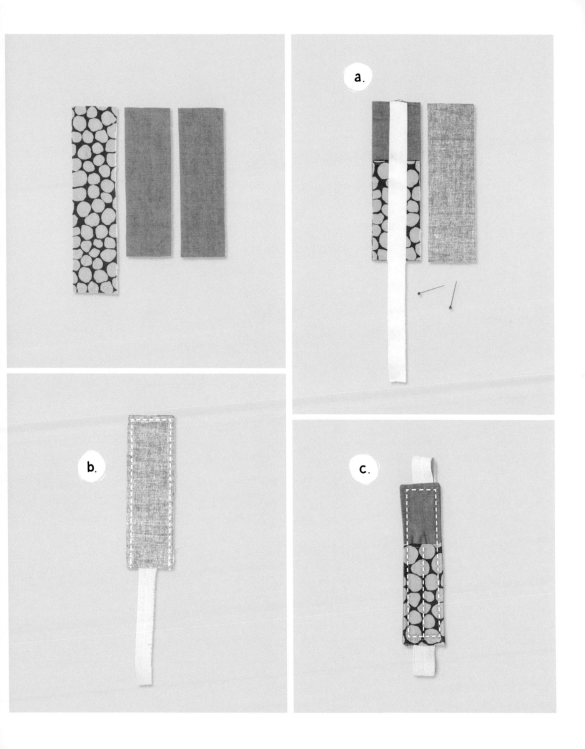

Art Organizer Case

The perfect gift for organizing your creative friends, this fabric case will keep together all their pens, pencils and brushes in one coordinated place. Why not fill it with art supplies before you wrap it up, for an extra-special surprise.

HOW TO MAKE

Materials

2 pieces of fabric, 45cm x 25cm (18in x 10in) for the outer and inner

1 piece of fabric, 45cm x 28cm (18in x 11in) for the pocket

Fusible interfacing, 45cm x 25cm (18in x 10in)

Ribbon, 50cm (20in)

Ruler (optional)

Sewing machine

Pins

1. Take the fabric that's going to be your inner section and iron the fusible interfacing to the underside.

2. Take your pocket material and fold in half length-wise and iron. Now topstitch along the folded edge. (See photo 'a' overleaf.)

3. Place your folded pocket section on top of the inner fabric (right side up), lining up the bottom raw edges. Pin in place. (See photo 'b' overleaf.)

4. On the other side of the inner fabric (the fusible webbing side), mark out your pockets with a pencil and ruler. It's best to draw yourself a template for this, marking out the sections (see photo 'c' overleaf) as shown. If you have a fabric pen, you can draw on the pocket side, of course, but it's easier to draw on the fusible interfacing side.

5. Now stitch along the lines you have drawn to divide the pocket into sections for pencils and a notebook. Remember to backstitch at the beginning and the end and trim all the loose thread. (See photo 'd'.)

6. Cut your ribbon in half and pin one half to the left-hand side and one to the right, at the point that the top of the pocket meets the inner fabric. The ribbon will be pointing towards the centre of the fabric. Stitch the outer edge in place (see photo 'e').

7. With the inner fabric and pocket section facing up, place the outer piece of fabric on top, right side down (so that they are right sides together) and stitch all the way round with a 1cm (½in) seam allowance. Leave a 10cm (4in) gap at the top for turning right side out. Make sure that your ribbon stays in the middle and doesn't get caught in the stitching.

8. Cut the corners of the fabric and then turn right side out, carefully turning out the corners with a pencil.

9. Iron flat and then topstitch all the way around the edge to give a neat finish and to close the gap.

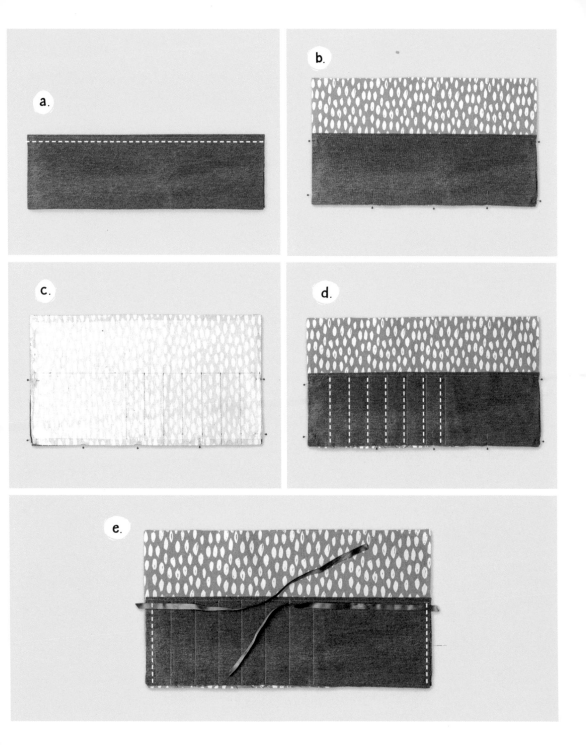

Travel Folder

Wanderlust friends will love to receive this
thoughtful and useful eco-friendly travel
wallet stitched with kindness and care.

HOW TO MAKE

Materials

3 different types of
fabric cut as follows:

Fabric 1 (patterned):
1 piece 25cm x 30cm
(10in x 12in) and 2 pieces
15cm x 12cm (6in x 5in)

Fabric 2 (yellow): 2 pieces 15cm
x 25cm (6in x 10in), 2 pieces
15cm x 20cm (6in x 8in)

Fabric 3 (coral): 1 piece 25cm
x 30cm (10in x 12in), 2 pieces
15cm x 25cm (6in x 10in)

Length of elastic, 25cm (10in)

Sewing machine

1. Take a piece of the 15cm x 12cm fabric 1 and a
   piece of the 15cm x 20cm fabric 2 and hem the
   longer edge of fabric 1 and the shorter edge of
   fabric 2 (these are the top edges of both).

2. Lay both pieces on top of the 15cm x 25cm piece of
   fabric 3, right sides up (see photo 'a'), and then take
   a 15cm x 25cm piece of fabric 2 and put that on
   top so the right sides are together (i.e. the sides you
   want to be visible are currently hidden). Stitch all the
   way down the right-hand side of this (see photo 'b')
   and then flip the top layer (fabric 2) to the back, so
   the wrong sides are together, and iron flat.

3. Now top stitch all the way down the right hand-
   side, which you have just pressed flat. This completes
   the left-hand side of your travel wallet, so repeat
   steps 1–3 for the right-hand side of your wallet, but
   this time, stitch all the way down the left-hand side
   before you flip the top layer. Press and top stitch the
   left side again.

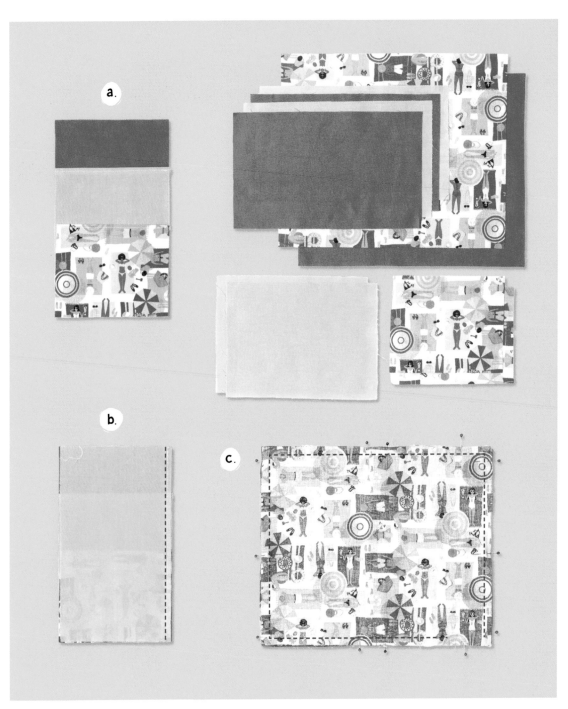

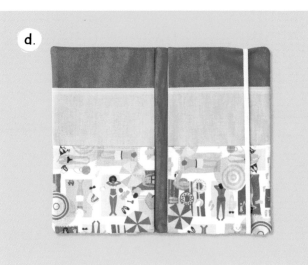

d.

TIP

*Why not fill the wallet
with keepsakes collected
from a special holiday with
a partner or friend as a
thoughtful personal
present.*

4. Take the 25cm x 30cm piece of fabric 3 and place it right side up. Now take your right and left side pockets of your wallet on top of that, right side up. Line up your edges and corners. Lay your piece of elastic on top, vertically, on the right-hand side, about 4cm (1½in) from the outer edge.

5. Lay the 25cm x 30cm piece of fabric 1 on top of this, right side down and pin in place. Stitch around all the edges but leave a small 5cm (2in) gap so you can turn it the right side out. (See photo 'c'.)

6. Turn it the right way out and then iron flat. Top stitch around the outside edges, tucking in the opening seam so it's neat, and being careful about not sewing the elastic. (See photo 'd'.)

Tassel Key Ring

Colourful and quirky, this tassel key ring is both simple
to make and a distinctive addition to a plain handbag.
Perfect for a friend who is always losing their keys.

HOW TO MAKE

Materials

Cotton cord, 22cm
(9in) long and around
4–6mm (¹/₄ in) thick

Split-ring key ring and
connecting loop or chain

Embroidery thread (aim for
3 or 4 different colours)

Embroidery needle

Washi tape

Pencil

Pliers (optional)

1. Take your cotton cord and fold it in half; stick a needle across the middle to keep it still during steps 1 and 2. Individually wrap the ends that will become the tassels in a bit of washi tape and attach the split-ring key ring into the top of the cord (you might want to use pliers to open and close the connecting loop).

2. With a pencil, mark about 5cm (2in) from the ends of the cord as your starting and ending points. This is where you will start and stop winding your thread.

3. Remove the needle, then take your first colour thread and start wrapping it round. If you lie the end of the thread down the length of your cord above the start point then it will be tucked away neatly and securely as you will eventually cover it up as you wrap over it.

4. Change colour thread as many times as you like, making sure the ends of the new and old thread are always secured by wrapping the new colour over the top. When you get to the key ring, wrap as close as you can to it so there is no white showing through.

5. Keep wrapping colours around until you get to your marked end point (both sides should be equal). Now, take a new colour thread to wrap around both ends together to form a loop. Aim for about 1cm or a half-inch thickness of wrapping.

6. Take your needle and thread it with the end of the yarn you have just been using. Sew back and forth through the cotton cord until the end wrap is secure.

7. Take off the tape from the ends and, using a comb or your fingers, separate all the strands of the cord to form your tassel. Trim any odd lengths so you have a neat finish.

TIP

Try using an embroidery skein instead of cord for a mini tassel (see far left key ring).

Lavender Soy-Wax Candle

Rainbow Tassel Hanging

Log Coasters

Unique Utensils

Centrepiece Classics

Flying Flags

Hanging Hearts

Heart on a String

Our loved ones should be celebrated at every opportunity and this collection of gifts will help to inspire creative ways to say 'thank you' as well as making any party look Instagram-worthy.

The lavender soy-wax candle will look perfect on any dinner table and can help to create a calming sanctuary for a stressed-out friend. Get creative with your pyrography pen kit to make some unique artwork coasters for those moving into a new home and in need of often-forgotten essentials. And why not gift some decorated utensils to a budding chef wanting to look the part?

For a dinner party in need of a little cheer, the centrepiece classics will make any table feel sumptuous. And the flying flags accessory is the perfect finishing touch to make your party feel like a real celebration. Though you won't want to save them just for special occasions: they're perfect for zinging up a home office space or as a cool focal point above your bed.

Celebration

Lavender
Soy-Wax Candle

This natural homemade candle makes for a pretty ornament as well as a sweet-smelling present: an ideal gift on both counts! Experiment with a range of dried flowers and essential oils to make a variety of deliciously-scented countryside candles.

HOW TO MAKE

Materials

An old glass jar (ours was 320ml, or 11 fl oz)

300g (11oz) soy wax

10–15 drops of lavender essential oil

A few springs of fresh or dried lavender

15cm (6in) pre-tabbed candle wick

Peg

1. Take your lavender and press between two heavy books until the heads are very flat and completely dry (this will probably take a few days). Trim the stems so that they sit about 2.5cm (1in) below the rim of your jar.

2. Place a saucepan of water over a medium heat and put a heatproof bowl over the top. Add your soy wax to the bowl and let it melt completely.

3. Take a sprig of lavender and carefully dip it into the melted wax before placing in your jar so that it sticks to the glass sides. You can use an old paintbrush to spread a bit of the wax over the lavender and glass to hold it in place. Place all your lavender around the inside of the jar in the same way.

4. Take one of your candle wicks and put it into the jar with the tab in the centre at the bottom. Take a peg and balance it across the top of the jar so that it holds the wick in place.

5. Add the essential oil to the pot of melted wax and stir well. If it looks like it's solidified, you can reheat it. Now transfer it into the jar. Leave it to set for forty-eight hours and then, once cured, trim the wick.

TIP

Try using the recipient's favourite flowers or herbs to decorate the candle — just make sure they're completely dry before you start.

Rainbow Tassel Hanging

Bring some joy with this colourful rainbow hanging,
which can be easily adapted to use whatever leftover
wool you have at home. Have fun experimenting
with different sizes of your rainbow arches and the
combination of shades to brighten a blank wall space.

HOW TO MAKE

Materials

Cotton rope, 1cm (½in)
thick. For an outer/upper
rainbow arch of approximately
65cm (25in) you will need
2.5m (8ft 2in) in total

A ball of organic cotton
yarn for each arch of the
rainbow – whichever
colours make you happy!

Needle

Washi tape

Thin wire – just less than the
length of the cotton rope

1. Cut a piece of cotton rope to be the size of your top arch. You can make this as big or as small as you want, though just bear in mind that if you make it too small you might not be able to fit many arches underneath it, and the bigger the arch the more yarn you will need.

2. Now cut as many arches as you like to fit underneath (you don't have to stick to the traditional seven colours of the rainbow!) and then tape up the ends to stop them fraying at this point.

3. Mark with pencil where you are going to start and stop wrapping on your arches so that they are equal. Now cut the wire to a slightly shorter length than the space that is to be wrapped.

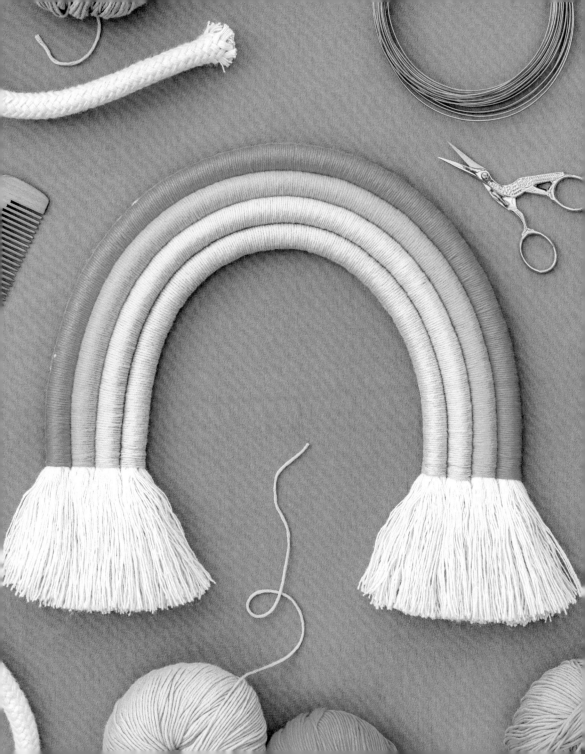

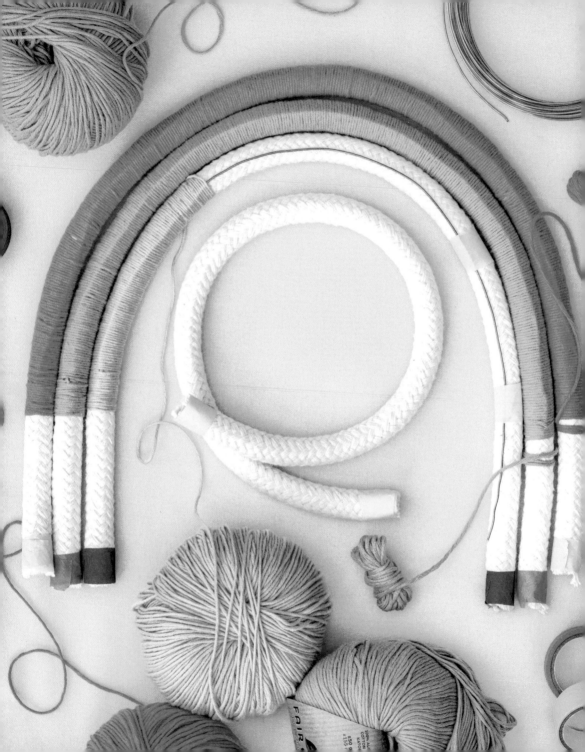

4. Take your wire and shape it to your first arch. Beginning at your marked point, wrap your wool or yarn around and around the arch and the wire together, trapping the end of your thread as you go to keep it secure. You need to bear in mind that this will be the back of the rainbow, so when wrapping make sure that the thread is neat on what will be the front once turned around.

5. Carry on wrapping until you reach the end mark. Wait to secure it until you have wrapped each arch, as you can always adjust the wrapping so it's even. Repeat for all of your arches. When you are happy that all the wrapping will be level when the arches are put together, sew the ends of the thread in through the rope and then trim so that it is hidden.

6. To attach all the arches together, take your needle and thread and sew down through all the wrapped ropes and back up again, in a zig-zag throughout the whole arch. Secure the end with a small knot or through the wrapped thread and sew in the end so it's hidden.

7. Sew a piece of embroidery thread or yarn in and out of the back of the second-from-top arch and tie it so it makes a small loop that will allow you to hang it on the wall.

8. To create the tassel effect, remove the tape from the ends of the rope, separate out the strands and trim to make them neat.

Log Coasters

The perfect resting place for a morning brew, this set of individually designed coasters make the ideal personalized present for house-proud recipients. Using pyrography, the art of decorating wood through burn marks made with a specially designed pen, you can create a design that's completely unique.

HOW TO MAKE

Materials

5 wood slices cut from fallen branches, around 10cm (4in) wide (if you don't have the tools to cut wood from branches, wood slices are available to buy cheaply online)

Pencil

Tracing paper

Pyrography pen kit

1. Draw around your wood slice on tracing paper and then draw out your design to the scale you want it to appear on the coaster.

2. Turn over the tracing paper and transfer the design onto the wood slice by rubbing the pencil over the top as a guide for your pyro pen.

3. Once your pen has heated up, start 'drawing' on the log with it, making sure to always keep the pen moving so it burns evenly over the surface.

4. If you find your design has become too darkly burnt and you want to lighten it, go over it lightly with a piece of sandpaper.

5. Repeat the process until you have a set of five. Try contrasting designs to make a truly unique set.

TIP

Always take care when using a pyrograph pen, as the nib gets very hot!

Unique Utensils

Spruce up someone's utensil jar with some prettily designed wooden tools that are both practical and unique. Using a pyrography pen kit, follow a natural theme with a leafy design or be creative and experiment with your own patterns to turn a plain wooden spoon into an unusual and welcome offering.

HOW TO MAKE

Materials

Wooden or bamboo utensils of your choice (spoons, salad tongs, spatulas, etc.)

Pencil

Tracing paper

Pyrography pen kit

Oil to finish (optional)

1. Trace around the utensil you are going to decorate and draw your design onto the paper. Or you can sketch out your design freehand and then draw over in pencil when you're happy with it.

2. Transfer your tracing-paper design onto your utensil as a guide for your pyro pen and then start burning the design on.

3. You can create a shiny, sleek finish by oiling your utensil with either walnut, olive, almond or linseed oil.

Centrepiece Classics

The joy of this elegant yet understated centrepiece is in its simplicity and adaptability to suit any occasion. You can adapt your centrepiece masterpiece to the types of glass containers you have and experiment with all sorts of foliage, mixing it up for any kind of stylish soirée.

HOW TO MAKE

Materials

White soy-wax candles

A few sprigs of eucalyptus (or other foliage – see what you can forage or find at your local florist)

Glass bottles, such as a clear wine bottle

1. Explore the great outdoors and gather your preferred foliage to fill the bottle. Eucalyptus is a great place to start, as it adds a dash of classic silvery green to this centrepiece, its fresh tone set off against the stark white candle.

2. Trim the cuttings to fit neatly inside your glass bottle. Don't overfill them – one or two stems depending on the size of your container will work.

3. Once you are happy with the amount inside, take your candle and shave the edges if needed so it fits snuggly into the top of the bottle.

4. Three glass bottles will make an eye-catching centrepiece that isn't too overpowering but adds a polished feel to the occasion.

Flying Flags

The joy of making this delightful decoration is equal to the joy of seeing it up: a constant, friendly reminder of recyclable craft. No home is complete without bunting and we don't mean just when an occasion calls for it. Whether it's pops of colourful flags for an exuberant friend or gentle, calming shades that complement a home office space, these handmade flags can be adapted to suit all.

▲ ▲ ▲ ▲ ▲

HOW TO MAKE

Materials

Scraps of material from anything you no longer use – old clothes, tablecloths, napkins, etc.

2m (6½ft) single-fold bias binding (or wide ribbon if you prefer)

Sewing machine or needle and thread

Pins

Scrap card or paper for template

1. Start by making a triangle template for your flags from card or paper – we used a triangle with a 12cm (4½in) base, measuring 12cm from base to point, but you can make whatever size you like. Pin the template to your fabric and cut round it. You will need fourteen triangles in total, for seven flags. Try to use your template as efficiently as possible on the fabric to reduce any waste.

2. Take two triangles and pin them right side (i.e. the sides you want to be visible) together. Repeat until all your triangles are pinned in pairs.

3. Sew or hand stitch along the edges of the flag 1cm (just under ½in) from the edge, starting from the top corner down towards the bottom point you have marked and then back up the other side. Don't sew along the top.

4. Trim the bottom 'point', being careful not to cut the stiches. Trim away some of the bulk at either side of the point, too. Then turn your pennant right side out and iron flat. You might need a chopstick or pencil to push out the point of your flag. Repeat steps 3 and 4 until all of them are completed.

5. Take your bias binding and lay it flat on a surface with the folded top and bottom facing upwards. Pin the top, unfinished edge of your first flag to the bottom fold of the bias tape, approximately 20cm (8in) from the end. Leave a gap of about 8cm (3in) before pinning your next flag. Continue until all your flags are pinned in place, equally spaced out.

6. Turn over the top flap of the bias binding, pin it in place over the raw edge of your flags and then sew along from one end to the other, making sure you are stitching through all the layers.

7. Fold over each end of the bias binding to create a small loop and stitch in place. Give your bunting one last iron before putting it up on show.

TIP

If you want to have more flags flying, you can decrease the gap between them or try larger or smaller flags – it's easy to personalize to suit your space.

TIP

These make an ideal individual wedding-day gift and can be adapted for other celebrations, too – you can use whatever shape you like.

Hanging Hearts

Create an everlasting token of affection with
these personalized ceramic hearts.

HOW TO MAKE

Materials

Air-dry clay

Rolling pin

Heart-shaped cookie cutter
(or try with other shapes, too)

Alphabet rubber stamps

1. Roll out a small quantity of clay (smaller than your fist) and keep rolling flat until it's about 0.5cm (less than ¼in) thick.

2. Take your heart cookie cutter and cut out three or four heart shapes. Using a craft knife or the lid of a pen, make two small holes in the top and one in the bottom of the first heart. Then add one hole at the top and bottom for the next hearts. The last heart will only need one hole in the top.

3. Take your alphabet letters and, pressing firmly, stamp the words of your choice into each clay heart.

4. Let the clay dry for one to two days or until it has turned completely white. To make a hanging loop in the top heart, tie a knot in some string or ribbon before threading through the holes and secure with a second knot. Then using more knotted string, attach the rest of your hearts.

Heart on a String

Spread the love with this unique piece of art that's therapeutic and simple to make. The size and colour of your finished heart will depend on the materials you have available, so go wild and experiment with lots of threads and ribbon.

HOW TO MAKE

Materials

Salvaged wood, ideally around 30cm x 20cm (12in x 8in) and rustic in look

Heart-shape template drawn on a piece of paper to fit on the wood

Small nails or tacks

Hammer

Coloured wool or thick thread

1. Place your paper template over the top of your piece of wood. You can make it any size you want – a smaller piece of wood works, too.

2. With your template in place, hammer your nails all around the shape of the heart. The nails don't need to go in too deep and don't worry about the paper, it will all come off at the end. Aim for about 1cm (just under ½in) spacing between each nail.

3. Once you have nails all the way around the template, rip off the paper, ensuring all the little bits are removed, leaving your nails in the shape of a heart on the wooden backing.

4. Take your wool or string and start by tying one end to the bottom of your heart before going all the way around your shape. When you get to the inverted point of the heart, go around the nail once before continuing around the outside.

5. Once you have completed an outline, take your wool from side to side, criss-crossing the shape in whatever direction you choose and wrapping round each nail as you go. There is no pattern to follow, just make sure you build your heart shape evenly.

6. When you have finished the inside, take your wool around the outside once more and then back to the bottom where you first tied the end and knot both ends securely, trimming any excess. If you want to hang your heart on the wall, you can add a hook on the back of the wood.

Tiny Paws Trinket Bowls

Vegan Dog Treats

Dog Chew Toy

Moggy Mouse Toy

Zero-waste gifts aren't just for two-legged recipients, you know. It might be easy to think that being green is only doable in certain areas of our lives, but when the best things in life are furry, you can extend your eco-conscious mantras to the fur-kids, too.

Animal lovers will appreciate the trinket bowls, which will be a cute accessory on their bedside table, while your canine-loving work colleagues will be sure to enjoy the T-shirt dog chew as a new toy for their pooch. And hey, it might just give the table legs a bit of rest-bite.

And let's not forget the moggy movers and shakers. The simple-to-make catnip mouse toy is a great way of finding a new use for old shirts (we're not kitten you, these things are worth keeping). Just watch your cat spring into action and attack.

And for a foodie treat with a difference, the vegan dog biscuits are a jar full of yumminess to bestow on any dog-lover's mutt. You might not get a thanks, but a wag of a tail speaks much louder than words.

Pet Presents

Tiny Paws
Trinket Bowls

Give your pet-loving pal a reminder of their furry friend
with this super-cute trinket bowl, perfect for jewellery or
keepsakes. It's the ideal present for your animal-loving
neighbour or your feline-obsessed mum, keeping both
your two-legged and four-legged friends happy.

HOW TO MAKE

Materials

Air-dry clay

Small bowl with shallow
sides to use as a mould

Rolling pin

Pencil and paper

Craft knife

Sandpaper

Coloured pencils

1. Take the bowl that you are using as a mould, turn
it upside down and draw around it on your paper.
Inside the circle, sketch the outline of the design
you want, e.g. the animal's face and ears. Cut out
your template.

2. Take out a fist-full of clay and roll it out until it's
approximately 0.5cm (under ¼ in) thick. Turn the
clay each time you roll to keep the thickness even.

3. Put your template on top of the clay and cut
around it with your craft knife. Remove any excess
clay before carefully placing it inside the bowl and
gently pressing down until it touches the bottom
and the sides, using a wet finger to smooth away
any wrinkles or uneven parts.

4. Allow it to dry for two or three days before carefully popping your clay bowl out of the original bowl. Use the sandpaper to smooth away any rough surfaces. (Make sure you do this step outside or by a window so you don't inhale any clay dust.)

5. Draw on your design using the coloured pencils.

TIP

If you have any old acrylic paints lying around, you can use them instead of pencils – but don't buy any new paints, as they aren't very eco!

TIP

Remember, these are tasty treats, so the lucky dog should only eat one or two per day.

Vegan Dog Treats

These vegan biscuits are the perfect delicacy
for the furry friends in your life.

HOW TO MAKE

Materials

*(makes approx. 12 treats, depending
on the size of your cutter)*

130g (1 cup) of wholegrain
flour (or oat or rice flour if
your dog is sensitive to gluten)

2 ripe bananas

80g (¼ cup) of smooth
organic peanut butter (make
sure it is dog-safe and
doesn't contain xylitol)

Rolling pin

Dog-bone cookie
cutter or knife

Baking tray

Baking paper

1. Peel the bananas and mash with the peanut butter in a bowl until it is all mixed together and smooth.

2. Add in half of the flour and mix until it is all combined and then add in the remaining flour and mix again.

3. Using your hands, bring the dough together into a ball and place on a well-floured surface. Roll out the mixture until it is about 1cm (½ inch) thick. You can add more flour as you go if it begins to stick.

4. Using a bone-shaped cookie cutter or a knife, cut out as many shapes as you can and transfer them to a baking tray lined with baking paper. Bring together any scraps and roll out again until you are out of dough.

5. Use a fork to make four holes in the centre of each bone to allow steam to escape. Pop in an oven preheated to 160°C (320°F) and bake for thirty minutes. Once cooled, store in an air-tight glass jar.

Dog Chew Toy

Looking for a cheap and eco-friendly way of spoiling your dog with a new toy? This unique chew requires minimum effort and materials to make but it will receive maximum tail wags in gratitude. And human tails would wag too if you wrapped and sent one to all your dog-owner acquaintances.

HOW TO MAKE

Materials

2 or 3 old T-shirts, depending on how colourful you would like the toy to be

Fabric scissors

TIP

You can make these chew toys from other bits of old fabric, but make sure the fabric is clean and doesn't easily fray.

1. Take one of your T-shirts and cut long strips from it, approximately 5–7cm (2–3in) wide. Do the same with your other T-shirts until you have eleven, fourteen or seventeen strands, depending on the desired thickness of the finished toy.

2. Gather all but two of your strips together and, using one of the spare strips, tie off one end about 5cm (2 inches) from the top.

3. Separate your T-shirt strips into three equal parts and start plaiting. Once you are almost at the end, take the second spare strip and tie it around the end. Trim away any straggly bits of thread or material.

Moggy Mouse Toy

A simple yet purrfect toy that makes good use of old
shirts, tops or jackets, these handmade fabric mice
will go down a treat with your feline friends.

HOW TO MAKE

Materials

Scraps of hard-wearing
material like corduroy,
suit fabric, shirts, etc

Needle

Embroidery thread

Fusible interfacing

Iron

Stuffing (use strips of
the leftover shirt fabric
as an eco-alternative)

Dried catnip (optional)

Regular white string

1. Trace and transfer the blue pieces shown on the
    next page to make a template to cut your fabric.

2. Cut out the bottom section and one of the side
    pieces. Flip the side template over and cut out
    another piece for the other side of the mouse.

3. To make the tail, plait three strands of white string
    and tie a knot at both ends. Make the tail around
    7cm (3in) long. For the ears, choose two bits of fabric
    and use the fusible interfacing to stick the pieces
    of fabric together. Then, using the ear template, cut out
    two ears from fused fabric.

4. Take both sides of the body fabric and pin the
    curved edges so that they are right sides (i.e. the
    sides you want to show on the outside) together.
    Pin the flat bottom edges to the bottom piece, so
    you have all three body pieces together, right sides
    facing. Insert and pin the tail into position (inside
    the pinned-together fabric, with only one knotted
    end outside).

TIP

Why not make a small batch to gift to local animal shelters or post to a favourite kitten-crazy friend. You'll be the cat's whiskers.

5. Sew around the edges with a 0.5cm (¼in) seam, ensuring you catch the tail to secure it, leaving a small gap at the back, next to the tail. Turn the body the right side out and stuff it. If you are using catnip, add in a little just before you sew it up.

6. Fold the ears in half and, using small stiches, attach them to the body. Take some thread (any thread will work) and backstitch two eyes and a nose onto the face.

Equipment

Making green gifts takes some patience and
preparation, so here are some tips and tricks to help
you on your way to creating your very own store
cupboard of planet-conscious tools and supplies.

▲ ▲ ▲ ▲ ▲

ECO-WRAPPING / Dig out scraps of material and reusable
fabric along with any old books, magazines or letters that will add an
air of mystery and romanticism to your wrapping. Keep old pieces of
string and ribbon stocked up, too, and invest in a hardy pair of fabric
scissors. For homemade cards, try to build up your stash of old cards
and washi tape as well as threads and yarn.

SUSTAINABLE HOME / Paintbrushes will come in useful
for making soy-wax wraps, along with a mix of fabric in different
patterns. Glass containers like gin bottles, old jam jars, etc. are
always great to have on hand. Keep a caddy of small nails/tacks as
well as string and rope in different lengths and widths.

PLANT POWER / Keep old plant pots, jars and containers and
have within easy reach basic tools such as pliers, sharp knives for
clay carving and sandpaper. You don't need to be green-fingered to
create any of these gifts – just a little care and attention for plants
goes a long way, as well as basic potting mix (and well-draining
succulent potting mix for succulents). Washi tape is useful for
making your plant gifts feel creatively presented, and keep an eye
out for good places to forage pretty foliage, too.

SELF-CARE TREATS / Build up a solid collection of essential oils so you can dip into preferred scents as you make these gifts. Don't be afraid to experiment with the ingredients you are using, either. A good set of weighing scales will be helpful as you create individual delights. Retain fabric that is hardwearing and pretty, and keep dried lavender, citric acid and bicarbonate of soda as well as old flannels and towels in your store cupboard, as they make brilliant eco-cleaning products. Likewise, keep any moisturizer tubs and used-up lip balm pots ready to refill.

ON THE GO / Fabric features heavily in this chapter, so if you have a sewing machine it will come in especially useful here. All the gifts can be hand sewn, too, so embroidery thread, needles, pins and time are also essential, as is a good pair of fabric scissors and a tape measure. If you're not already *au fait* with the sewing lingo, do seek out tutorials on YouTube – you'll be topstitching with the pros in no time. Do also keep any elastic bands and key chains.

CELEBRATION / Art essentials like pencils, tracing paper and rulers will come in handy, as will an artistic, creative flair. Large saucepans will be needed to dye bigger pieces of fabric. Have an iron and board ready to press fabric before you start, or the seams of your creations as you go. Soy wax, old jars, elastic bands, a pyrography pen, old glass bottles, air-dry clay, candles and rustic pieces of wood may also come in handy.

PET PRESENTS / Hardwearing material is best for these gifts if you want pets to enjoy them for as long as possible. Keep hold of jars with their lids so you can fill them with edible treats and know they are sealed and safe. Air-dry clay may be useful for pet-themed presents, and keep hold of old T-shirts, shirts and denim, too.